D0999802

4.95
80¢

EVALUATING RESEARCH PROPOSALS IN THE BEHAVIORAL SCIENCES:

A GUIDE

SECOND ENLARGED EDITION

JOEL ROBERT DAVITZ, Ph.D.
Professor of Psychology, Teachers College

LOIS LEIDERMAN DAVITZ, Ph.D.
Research Associate, Teachers College

TEACHERS COLLEGE PRESS
TEACHERS COLLEGE, COLUMBIA UNIVERSITY
NEW YORK AND LONDON

Originally published in 1967 as *A Guide for Evaluating Research Plans in Psychology and Education*; additional material has been added for this edition.

Copyright © 1967, 1977 by Joel R. Davitz, All rights reserved.
Published by Teachers College Press, 1234 Amsterdam Avenue, New York, NY 10027.

Library of Congress Cataloging in Publication Data
Davitz, Joel Robert.
    Evaluating research proposals in the behavioral
sciences.
    First ed. (1967) published under title: A guide for
evaluating research plans in psychology and education.
    Includes bibliographical references.
    1. Psychological research.   2. Educational research.
I. Davitz, Lois Jean, joint author.   II. Title.
BF76.5.D3   1977   301′.07′2   77-20296
ISBN 0-8077-2544-7

Manufactured in the United States of America

                                    3 4 5 6 7

BF
76.5
.D3
1977
c.3

CONTENTS

INTRODUCTION

This guide was prepared for students who are beginning to plan independent research studies. It is a summary of common points considered in evaluating a research proposal and is designed primarily as a framework within which a student might critically review his work.

By the time a student begins to plan his first independent investigation, he is likely to have had a certain amount of academic course work in measurement, statistics, and research methods. Thus, he probably is familiar with all the ideas contained in this guide. In working with our students, however, we have found that when a beginning researcher designs his own initial investigation, he sometimes neglects elementary aspects of research planning that he has learned about in previous course work. In fact, our experience suggests that problems in research planning more often involve straightforward and relatively obvious questions rather than subtle and complex problems of theory or design. For example, it is not uncommon for a student to present a proposal dealing with a difficult and significant problem in a most ingenious way, using an efficient and complex design, with intricate sampling procedures and careful concern with research controls, only to neglect a more obvious question regarding the reliability of the measures he plans to use. Perhaps these complex problems become "figure" simply because they are more difficult and challenging, but in any event, the task of preparing an original research plan might be eased by using a guide that systematically reviews problems commonly met in evaluating research proposals.

The problem areas included in this guide are derived from our experience in reviewing students' research proposals, and reflect our judgment of the most common problems encountered. Under each area, one or more specific questions are posed, each dealing with a somewhat different, although related, aspect of the general problem. Many of these problem areas are closely related to one another; in a more theoretical discussion of research methodology, several points in the guide would probably be treated under the same general heading because they concern essentially the same basic problem. Specific questions under each section sometimes are repeated from slightly different points of view and in somewhat different words. Thus, a certain amount of redundancy has purposefully been built into this book. On the basis of our own experiences, it seems wiser for the student at the outset of his research to consider the same basic problem from several perspectives, rather than to risk completing the study with a significant flaw that could have been circumvented in the initial planning stage.

In the main part of the book, each section includes a heading, one or more specific questions, and a brief explication of the general problem involved in that section. By and large, the explication for each section merely highlights and illustrates some of the major issues to be considered, and is designed to aid the student in recalling relevant material he has covered in previous reading and course work.

The second part of the guide presents a list of common research terms and concepts. Each term or concept is defined and illustrative examples are given.

Although this book has been prepared primarily for investigators who are beginning to develop their own research plans, it may also be useful for students who are learning to read and critically evaluate research publications. The problems encountered in devising a research proposal are essentially the same as those involved in the final publication; in a well-designed and carefully executed study, these problems have presumably been successfully resolved. Nevertheless, the same kinds of issues dealt with in planning must be considered in evaluating the final product; this book thus provides a framework within which to read research reports critically and knowledgeably.

In conclusion, the authors wish to thank the late Dean Laurance Shaffer and Professors Allen Bergin, Robert Thorndike, and Marvin Sontag for their critical reviews of various drafts of this guide.

JOEL ROBERT DAVITZ, Ph.D.
Professor of Psychology
LOIS LEIDERMAN DAVITZ, Ph.D.
Research Associate

Teachers College, Columbia University

CRITERIA
FOR EVALUATING
A RESEARCH PLAN

A CENTRAL THEME
• *What is the central logic or theme of the research? What is the core idea around which the investigation is organized, the thread of logic that starts with the first word of the proposal and carries through to the last word in the discussion of possible results?*

• *Is the central theme stated clearly and explicitly?*

• *Is the central theme stated early in the proposal and then carried through consistently to the end?*

If the proposal begins with a general discussion of intelligence, then reviews personality correlates of academic achievement, and ends with a paragraph devoted to an analysis of reading skills without tying these topics together in a clear, logical framework, then the proposed research is likely to be a fairly confused affair, and the proposal should be reworked.

Of course the research may also deal with ideas other than those directly involved in the central theme, but these should be treated as subsidiary to the main line of investigation, and the relation of these secondary ideas to the central theme should be spelled out clearly. In short, the proposal should state the central, major theme early and stick with it.

For further reference, see Ary, Jacobs, and Razavich, 1972, pp. 39–70.

THE CENTRAL THEME WITHIN A CONTEXT
• *What is the relation of the central theme of this study to other research and theory? Does the introduction to the study explicitly and clearly integrate the central logic of the proposed investigation within the broader framework of relevant theory and research?*

No research meaningfully stands alone. A single study may represent a major advance in an area of knowledge, but the advance always depends, at least in part, on empirical and theoretical inquiry that has gone before.

Not even the greatest figures of science—Newton, Darwin, Einstein—worked in an historical vacuum. Although single studies are written and published, these are always part of a *line of inquiry*, regardless of whether that line has been established explicitly in formal theory. Knowledge in a given area depends upon an interrelated series of investigations and a set of theoretical generalizations that are usually broader than those immediately involved in a single study. Thus, each study must be viewed within the context of a line of inquiry representing the cumulative development of knowledge about a given problem area.

Moreover, it is not enough simply to review mechanically an area of research or theory; a mere catalog of previous studies and theoretical statements does little to advance the argument of a research proposal if this material is not conceptually integrated within the logic of the proposed investigation. At each step, one must make explicit the relation between other work and the particular study being proposed.

For further reference, see Kerlinger, 1973, pp. 16–27.

SIMPLICITY, CLARITY, AND PARSIMONY

• *Is the proposal written as simply, clearly, and parsimoniously as possible?*

Many proposals, of course, involve complex ideas that require complex statements; but can the writing in the proposal be simplified in any way so that clarity of communication is enhanced? One of the dangers of thinking, writing, and doing research in a specialized area of inquiry is the jargon one can easily slip into. There is nothing wrong with specialized technical terms; in fact, investigators in most fields have to develop their own vocabulary for communicating accurately with each other about phenomena not adequately defined in the common language. But the eventual intellectual aim of research is simplicity and parsimony, and this should govern the style of writing. Mathematics represents the epitome of this stylistic goal, but even if a study cannot be formulated in mathematical symbols, at least the verbal presentation can aim at the simplicity, precision, and elegance of a mathematical formulation. If the researcher proposes "to utilize the discursive symbolization system of Anglo-American discourse," it would be better for him "to use the English language."

For further reference, see Barzun and Graff, 1977, pp. 228–261.

LOGICAL CONSISTENCY

• *Does the introduction lead logically and consistently to the specific questions posed or the hypotheses presented?*

The questions or hypotheses of a research represent a step beyond current knowledge. If this were not the case, there would be little sense in doing the research. Its purpose is to carry a line of inquiry forward, beyond what is already known. Thus research always involves something of a leap from the present state of knowledge, and occasionally this leap, in the form of research questions or hypotheses, may not be based clearly on the preceding introduction. Perhaps the logic relating previous work to the specific aims of the research has not been spelled out; perhaps the introduction, which might be adequate in itself, is not validly related to the specific questions or hypotheses posed. In any event, there is always a gap between previous work and the immediate research, and this gap must be bridged explicitly and logically.

RESEARCHABLE QUESTIONS AND HYPOTHESES
  • *Are the questions or hypotheses researchable? That is, can the questions be answered on an empirical basis? Can the hypotheses be tested by empirical data?*

The kinds of questions that can be investigated empirically are obviously limited. There are many questions that people feel are important but cannot be answered only on the basis of empirical data. These are questions involving value judgments, and they demand answers that are, to some extent, expressions of evaluative opinions. "Should the reduction of tension be the primary goal of psychotherapy?" "Should education be designed to foster creativity?" These are important questions, in that one's answers are likely to make a difference in psychotherapeutic practice or in planning an educational curriculum. But they are questions of value, and although empirical information might be useful in thinking about them, they demand answers that are statements of opinion, which to a certain degree are independent of facts. At the outset, therefore, the researcher must recognize that in his research he can deal directly only with questions that can be answered on the basis of empirical observations.
For further reference, see Best, 1977, pp. 5–15.

SPECIFICITY OF QUESTIONS AND
OPERATIONAL DEFINITIONS
  • *Are the questions or hypotheses specific enough to be investigated?*
  • *Are the variables under investigation and the nature of the relationships among variables clearly and concretely stated?*
  • *Can every term in the questions or hypotheses be referred either directly or indirectly to observable, empirical events? Do the*

variables stated in the questions or hypotheses refer to a particular set of internally consistent observations that are capable of being defined operationally and objectively?

Several sections in this guide concern the statement of questions or hypotheses in a research proposal, each section dealing with a somewhat different aspect of the same general problem. So much emphasis has been given to this phase of a proposal because the rest of any proposed study derives from the initial formulation of one's questions or hypotheses. Asking the right question in the right way to a large degree determines the value of a research and therefore is one of the most important steps any investigator takes in planning his research.

A problem frequently encountered by beginning researchers is the magnitude of questions that can feasibly be investigated at a given time within the practical limits of available resources. "Is psychotherapy effective?" "What kinds of child rearing practices lead to the development of psychological maladjustment?" "How can a teacher most effectively foster student learning?" In a broad sense, all these questions identify domains within which research is possible, and probably all these questions are important to investigate. But they are the kinds of questions that are gradually answered by an accumulation of knowledge obtained in many studies conducted by numerous investigators over a substantial period of time. They are *not* questions that are answered by a single study, no matter how incisive or crucial.

A mark of the mature, productive researcher is the capacity to focus his or her research questions at a concrete level of specificity, which permits him or her to get on with the problem at hand. Of course, he or she must relate the particular investigation to a broader line of inquiry, but he or she also must limit the study in a realistic way. One cannot expect to evaluate all aspects of psychotherapy, but one can study the effects of certain aspects of therapy on specific behaviors manifested by particular kinds of patients. One cannot reasonably hope to discover the most effective teaching techniques for all teachers, all students, all subject matter, in all situations; but one can determine the effect of a particular teaching technique used by certain kinds of teachers with certain kinds of students studying a given body of subject matter.

For further reference, see Kerlinger, 1973, pp. 28–47.

HYPOTHESIS TESTING, HYPOTHESIS GENERATING, AND DESCRIPTIVE RESEARCH

• *In view of the current state of knowledge in a given line of inquiry, is the most profitable study at this point likely to be: (a) a est of specific hypotheses; (b) exploratory, perhaps generating a hypothesis; or (c) descriptive? Is the proposed research plan consistent with one's opinion about the kind of research that currently seems most likely to be profitable?*

• *If the investigation has primarily an exploratory or descriptive purpose, is every reasonable effort made to present the limits of the questions posed, to make as concrete and definite as possible the nature of relevant observations and variables to be studied?*

In some instances, particularly early in a line of investigation, the major purpose of research is exploratory or descriptive, and the central question of a study must necessarily be somewhat open-ended, because the terms of the answer to such a question cannot be fully anticipated before the observations are made. In the opinion of some investigators, many areas in psychological or educational theory and research have not yet reached a level of sophistication at which it is profitable and appropriate to design studies involving tests of highly refined and specific hypotheses. Regardless of one's opinion on this matter, probably most investigators in psychology and education would agree that relatively few studies in the past have turned out to be crucial tests of hypotheses that have had great theoretical or practical import. This general issue will be dealt with in the next sections of this guide, which concern the meaningfulness of a proposed research and with the choice of strategy in research. At this point, the more general problem may be viewed in terms of the way in which the central questions or hypotheses of a study are formulated. From this perspective, probably few psychologists or educators would argue against the current need for exploratory, hypothesis-generating, and descriptive studies.

In planning this kind of research, however, the investigator must take great care to make explicit the logic of the study, the limits of the investigation, the concrete guideposts of the observations, and the variety of possible terms in which he or she may find relevant answers to the initial questions.

Exploratory and descriptive studies are the most difficult kinds of research to do well. In most respects, it is easier to formulate a specific hypothesis and design a study simply to test that hypothesis, because the researcher usually is not required to go very far beyond what is already known. But in an exploratory study, there is an implicit demand for discovery, and success often depends upon a certain amount of luck as well as technical skill and diligence. For certain problem areas, perhaps the descriptive parameters have not yet been defined, and the researcher may be required to develop the basic vocabulary and grammar for describing the phenomena under investigation. Therefore, although exploratory, hypothesis-generating, and descriptive studies might well be encouraged in many

areas of psychology and education, it is also important to recognize tha
success in this kind of research depends upon the way in which the basi
questions are formulated and the care with which relevant observations an
potentially important variables are delineated.

For further reference, see Ary, Jacobs, and Razavich, 1972, pp. 213-
306.

MEANINGFUL QUESTIONS AND HYPOTHESES

• *Are the possible findings of the research likely to make a differ
ence that counts in terms of theory, other research, or any practica
issue? Thus, is the research worth doing?*

• *In the light of current knowledge, does the proposed researcl
deal with an appropriate problem, a question or hypothesis that i
likely to carry the general line of investigation forward? Are ther
other questions that should be investigated before the proposed prob
lem is confronted? Has this problem essentially been resolved ir
earlier research?*

Investigators in the social sciences have sometimes been accused o.
dealing largely with the obvious or the trivial, and there is probably som
validity in this accusation. In an effort to maximize the rigor of one's re
search, there frequently is a temptation to focus on questions that can b
treated neatly and precisely within the well-controlled conditions of a lab
oratory. But the most clear, precise, and elegant research question may be
meaningless if an answer to this question makes no difference for theory
for other research, or for practice. Certainly some important questions a
the present time can be attacked meaningfully under the most rigorou
laboratory conditions, but if amenability to neatness and precision of in
vestigation becomes the only major criterion for selecting a research prob
lem, there is a real danger of being lost in trivia.

In view of the cumulative nature of scientific inquiry, one must also
attend to the appropriate timing in investigating a particular problem. Fo
example, it would probably not be very profitable to launch an investigatior
of possible correlates of creativity before an adequate measure of creativity
has been developed. Often, rigorously controlled experimental research can
not be done effectively in a given area until more fundamental descriptive
work has been done in establishing the basic parameters to be investigated
The productive researcher usually has a keen sense of timing, in that he o
she has the capacity to formulate the right question at the right time, the
question that will make a significant difference in a line of inquiry. There
are no rigid criteria by which to guide the formulation of these questions.
As a beginning, however, one can at least ask if any possible answer to the

question posed for investigation is likely to result in a difference of any
import. For further reference, see Carlsmith, Ellsworth, and Aronson, 1976,
pp. 86–92.

STRATEGY OF THE INVESTIGATION

* Has the researcher chosen an appropriate overall strategy for his or her investigation?

There are many ways of classifying strategies of research, but one
common classification divides these strategies into three general groups:
(1) natural observation, (2) correlational studies, and (3) experimental
manipulation.

Suppose an investigator is interested in studying the educative process
of a primitive culture about which he has little information. He or she
knows that the culture has been transmitted from one generation to another,
but doesn't know very much about the situations in which this transmission
occurs, who is involved, or how the process takes place. It would probably
be inappropriate for him or her to begin the investigations armed with a
battery of achievement tests devised for American children or rating scales
developed to study American college classrooms. Instead, the initial task
might well involve a substantial period of careful and comprehensive observation of the educative processes in this culture as they occur naturally,
without experimental control or manipulation. On the basis of these "natural
observations," he or she could then describe the general phenomena involved, define the major parameters to be investigated, and perhaps formulate the kinds of questions that are likely to be important in further
research. This kind of research typically doesn't provide the final answers
to most problems, but in most areas of inquiry it is a necessary first step
that cannot be disregarded in favor of other, more rigorously controlled
strategies. As a matter of fact, in the social and behavioral sciences, some
have argued that not enough of this kind of research has been done and
that therefore many investigators have dealt with the wrong problems or
have floundered in trivia.

There are many problems, however, about which enough is known to
design meaningful correlational studies. In these instances, the aim is to
determine the relationships among variables as they occur "in nature,"
achieving research control through such means as selection of subjects or
assessment and statistical control of potentially relevant variables. Thus,
for example, an investigator might study the relation between verbal
intelligence and academic achievement as they co-occur in a given school
population, controlling by one means or another such variables as age,

sex, and socioeconomic status. Much of the research in the social science relies on this kind of strategy. The long psychometric tradition in psychology, for example, is representative of this tendency.

Incidentally, a "correlational strategy" does not necessarily mean that a correlation statistic (e.g., a rank order correlation) is used in the study. Many other statistics might be appropriate in such a study. The important point is that the investigator measures two or more variables and studies their relation to each other.

In many kinds of research, the variables involved cannot be manipulated, perhaps for humanitarian reasons, or because it is practically impossible. Thus, there are various theories about the kind of deprived childhood presumably associated with subsequent development of schizophrenia, but for both humanitarian and practical reasons, no researcher is likely to create such child rearing conditions for experimental purpose and systematically rear children with the aim of inducing schizophrenia. In dealing with this kind of problem, we must use a correlational strategy studying, for example, various child rearing conditions as they occur *in vivo* in relation to subsequent psychological adjustment.

This kind of research, of course, must use careful means of controlling relevant variables, but, even with the most adequate controls, the correlational strategy can lead only to a conclusion that variables *are* or *are not* related in a certain way. Correlational strategies cannot establish causality; that is, on the basis of a correlational study one cannot conclude that variable A is a necessary antecedent condition of variable B. This kind of conclusion depends upon the strategy of experimental manipulation.

The strategy of an experiment always involves systematic manipulation of one or more variables, usually called the independent variables, and measurement of the effect of this manipulation on one or more dependent variables. The experimenter might vary his or her responses to certain kinds of statements made by subjects during interviews and study the frequency of these statements as a function of the type of response made by the experimenter. For example, with one group of subjects, the experimenter might say "Mmhmm" every time a subject makes a statement beginning with the words, "I feel." In another group, he or she might simply nod after the subject makes a statement beginning with "I feel." Then, he or she could compare the effect of saying "Mmhmm" versus nodding his head on the frequency with which people make statements beginning with the words, "I feel." Or, an experimenter might devise two different sets of classroom conditions and compare their effects on measured changes in students' attitudes. Regardless of the particular area of research, the basic strategy of an experiment is controlled manipulation of one or more independent variables and the subsequent measurement of one or more dependent variables.

Many research problems call for a combination of strategies, often involving the use of both correlational and experimental models. For example, if one were interested in studying the effects of threat on learning, conditions of high and low threat could be experimentally manipulated. But it would be reasonable to expect that the effect of threat is a function of the amount of anxiety with which a subject came into the experimental situation. Thus, in addition to the experimental manipulation of threat, the investigator might also use a correlational strategy by obtaining a measure of each subject's initial anxiety. This information, then, might be extremely useful in clarifying the effects of the experimental manipulation.

There is obviously no single strategy that is "best" for all research, but, in every case, the choice of an appropriate research strategy determines to a large extent the value of any study that is done.

For further reference, see Best, 1977, pp. 90–146.

LOGIC AND VALIDITY OF RESEARCH PROCEDURES

• *Is the method a clearcut, logical extension of the central theme of the research?*

• *Can the method reasonably be expected to result in information that will answer the questions posed?*

• *Do the research procedures, such as the ways in which an independent variable is manipulated or in which the dependent variable is measured, provide a valid test of the hypotheses?*

Designing the procedures of a research involves a jump from words and concepts to empirical operations. The ideas developed in the introduction and focused in the research questions or hypotheses must be translated into events that are valid referents of these ideas. For example, an investigator may wish to study the effects of certain kinds of frustration on aggression, and there certainly is a substantial body of theoretical literature from which a variety of predictions might be made. But regardless of what hypotheses or questions are formulated, in designing a study the investigator must explicitly, logically, and validly translate the words "frustration" and "aggression" into the operations of the research procedure.

In many areas, certain methods of investigation have already been established in previous work, and it is usually wise to use these methods whenever possible and appropriate. Devising new methods simply to demonstrate one's own ingenuity is a disservice to oneself and others, because it is one more factor that tends to disrupt the consistency and cumulative power of a line of inquiry. However, there are also occasions in which new methods must be developed for the purposes of a particular study. Whatever the case may be—whether the method is completely original, an adaptation of preceding work, or totally based on previous research—the actual research procedures must be a valid translation of the logic of the research into observable, empirical events.

For further reference, see Carlsmith, Ellsworth, and Aronson, 1976, pp. 53-85.

PRACTICAL LIMITS AND REALISTIC CONSIDERATIONS

• *Is the method practical within the realistic limits in which the researcher must work? Has he or she considered the availability of subjects, the amount of time required for observations, the money required for various procedures, and other aspects of the real world in which he or she works? Once this has been done, can the researcher be expected to accomplish the procedures proposed?*

• *Is the researcher adequately trained to carry out the procedures?*

• *Are the methods consistent with the abilities of the subjects in the sample?*

Many potentially important studies haven't been done simply because of practical limitations the researcher inevitably encounters. Long-term longitudinal studies, for instance, are extremely important in developing and testing a variety of theories about human development, but such studies are rare because most researchers would find it difficult, if not practically impossible, to devote the 10, 20, or 30 years required to collect data.

Time, of course, is only one factor; money, equipment, cooperation, and availability of subjects are a few of the other realistic factors that must be considered, and although no general rule can be applied to every study, obviously a proposal must be within the realistic limits of the particular researcher in his particular situation.

Just as one would not want a surgeon to perform an operation for which he or she has not been trained, one would not want a researcher to use methods of investigation that he or she has not been adequately trained to use with precision and understanding. Interviewing involves much more than merely asking questions and taking down answers; using tests effectively requires a great deal of knowledge beyond knowing how to hand out answer sheets efficiently. No research is better than the methods that are used, and one obvious requisite of an acceptable research plan is the investigator's competence in the methods he or she proposes to use.

From another point of view, the methods of a research must be within the range of competence that can reasonably be expected among subjects in the sample. If the research requires subjects to answer a questionnaire, the vocabulary used in the questions must be phrased so that they are readily understood; otherwise, the research becomes an exercise in subjects' guessing about what is required. If a test is too easy or too hard for a given sample, the range of scores will probably be too restricted to permit any meaningful investigation. If an experimental procedure is particularly boring or too difficult for the subjects, these characteristics of the procedure itself will influence the results obtained and perhaps contaminate the interpretation of one's findings.

THE POPULATION AND THE SAMPLE

• *What is the population of subjects sampled? Are the pertinent characteristics of this population clearly stated?*

• *Does the researcher show adequate awareness of the limits of generalizations he or she can make on the basis of the research?*

An elementary principle of research is that one can generalize only to the population that is sampled. But probably no other single principle has been violated more often in discussions of research results. Having sampled a limited universe of American, white, middle-class, college students, many writers discuss their findings as if they applied to all mankind. Little can probably be done in the research proposal to protect against this danger in the final report, but at least the researcher can be explicit about the population sampled and his or her sampling procedures. This can serve, perhaps, as a reminder to the researcher of the appropriate limits to which he or she can legitimately generalize the results.

For further reference, see Nunnally, 1975, pp. 42-46.

SAMPLE SIZE

• *Is the size of the sample appropriate? In deciding on sample size, has the researcher considered relevant issues, such as the probable variability among subjects in the sample and the amount of variance likely to be accounted for by the variables under consideration?*

Many factors influence a decision about sample size. For example, if highly precise and reliable measures are used, other things being equal, a researcher might legitimately use a relatively small sample and have considerable confidence in the generality of the results. On the other hand, some studies are condemned to null results from the outset, because consistent findings with gross instruments currently available would require large samples that are realistically impossible to obtain.

In any sample, the likely range of a particular variable might be so small that it is unlikely one could obtain consistent findings without studying a very large number of subjects. Consider, for example, the relation between mental age and spelling ability of children who are within one month of being exactly twelve years old. The mental age of all children of a particular chronological age does vary, but if a researcher were to select his or her sample of children from a suburban school in a socioeconomically homogeneous neighborhood, he or she would probably have to study a very large sample indeed to discover a consistent, statistically reliable relationship between the two variables under consideration. If the sample consisted of only 20 or 30 children, the researcher would most likely obtain null results, simply because in this kind of sample, mental age probably would not vary enough to obtain a statistically significant correlation different from zero. Thus, the sample size must be consistent with the variability of the measures likely to be found.

Some variables might be related to a phenomenon in which the researcher is interested, but this relationship might be so tenuous or account for so little of the variance in the central phenomenon that an unrealistic sample size would be required to establish the relationship statistically. For example, eye color may be one variable that influences one's self concept. But among the hundreds of other variables that are likely to have greater influence on the self concept, eye color probably accounts for so little of the variance that a sample of thousands of subjects probably would be required to discover any consistent relationship involving eye color and self concept. In general, at the outset of an investigation the researcher might ask: What order of magnitude or relationship can one reasonably expect a particular factor to produce? Then, given the precision of measurement techniques used, what size sample is needed to detect this if it does occur? Thus, one can work a "back solution" to establish an appropriate sample size, and it is obviously wiser to arrive at this solution before a study begins than to depend on luck, convenience, or convention.

For further reference, see Kerlinger, 1973, pp. 127-129.

SAMPLING PROCEDURES
   • *Are appropriate methods of randomization and control used in selecting the sample?*
   • *Is the sample adequately described?*

In selecting subjects, the investigator is guided by two aims: (1) maintaining freedom from bias, and (2) maximizing the sensitivity of the research. He or she achieves these goals by appropriate use of both randomization and control in selecting the sample, deciding beforehand which of a variety of sampling techniques most efficiently satisfies the demands of the research.

In regard to many variables, the aim may be to select subjects so that there is no systematic influence that determines whether a subject is selected or to which of the research groups a subject is assigned. The aim is to assure *freedom from bias*, and assuming that the sample size is sufficiently large, the researcher would then depend upon random sampling techniques.

On the other hand, if it is reasonable on the basis of theory or previous research to expect that certain variables are likely to influence the particular phenomenon under investigation, the researcher would aim to increase the sensitivity of his investigation by using one or more means of sampling control. He might select subjects on the basis of explicit criteria, perhaps using stratified random samples, with appropriate matching or equating of groups. Or he might measure relevant variables within a random sample and then use appropriate statistical techniques to achieve control. In many studies of academic achievement, for instance, intelligence and social class of the subjects have accounted for a substantial portion of the variance in achievement. Therefore, to increase the sensitivity of work in any investigation of academic achievement, the investigator would want to control social class and intelligence, either by stratified sampling on the basis of explicit criteria or by assessment and statistical techniques. Otherwise, the results of the research are likely to be confused by the influence of these variables.

In addition to achieving freedom from bias in selecting the sample and increasing the sensitivity of the research by various means of control, the investigator must also be concerned with discovering other possible subject variables that might be related to the results. At the outset, of course, the nature of any such discovery cannot be anticipated, but discovery is at least possible if the sample is fully described. There are certainly limits to the amount of information that can reasonably be obtained in any research. But, in planning a study, it is probably wise to remember that, other things being equal, the more information available about the sample, the greater the likelihood of discovering potentially important relationships.

For further reference, see Jacobson, 1976, pp. 36-53.

APPROPRIATENESS OF SAMPLE AND POPULATION
• *Are the appropriate subjects used for the research?*

The usual criterion for selecting subjects is availability, and this certainly is a valid practical consideration. One cannot study the personality of Russian capitalists if the population is not available, but availability is only one criterion. The kinds of subjects selected must also depend on the problem being investigated. If one wanted to study sex differences in aesthetic taste, the population of graduate students in fine arts probably would not be a good group to sample, unless this group were of special interest for the research, because sex differences as they affect a variable such as aesthetic taste are likely to be obscured by educational experiences among these graduate students. For further reference, see Kerlinger, 1973, pp. 119-131.

ETHICAL CONSIDERATIONS

* *Is the procedure ethical?*

Ethical considerations must be taken into account in all research, but especially in studies involving deception of subjects, inquiry into areas commonly accepted as matters of private concern, the use of stressful procedures, or the study of subjects who are in a distressed condition psychologically, physically, economically, or in any other respect. In the past, some researchers have been accused of being careless in their ethical consideration of subjects they have studied. Although some of the accusations were probably unwarranted, there have undoubtedly been instances in which researchers have not been sufficiently sensitive to the ethical implications of their work and have not taken adequate safeguards to protect subjects from possible harm. This does not refer only to physical pain or injury, of course, but involves any kind of harm a subject might encounter as a result of participating in research. No other area of research planning calls for greater care and judgment. Every step in the research plan must be reviewed in detail to make sure that the subject is appropriately protected, and if there is any risk, any degree of psychological or physical distress entailed in the research procedure, the investigator must be absolutely sure that subjects are properly informed and give consent to participating in the research. Although an investigator may choose to take some chances in other aspects of research planning for the sake of possible discovery of new knowledge, when a research plan is viewed from an ethical point of view, only the most stringent, conservative, and safest criteria are appropriate for evaluating the research. Various professional organizations, such as The American Psychological Association, have devoted a great deal of effort to establish general principles and a code of ethics to guide a researcher's decisions regarding these problems. Nothing, however, can substitute for careful, thoughtful, and humane judgment in these matters.

For further reference, see American Psychological Association Ad Hoc Committee on Ethical Standards in Psychological Research, 1973; United States Public Health Service, 1969.

POTENCY AND VALIDITY OF EXPERIMENTAL INPUT

* *In an experimental study, is the experimental manipulation potent enough to make a measurable difference in the dependent variable?*

• *What is the evidence that an experimental manipulation will have the effect it is theoretically expected to have?*

Sometimes there is a perfectly sound theoretical basis for expecting one variable to be related to another in a consistent fashion, but an experiment may fail to demonstrate the relationship because the experimental input is too trivial or too weak to make any difference in behavior. For example, many kinds of rewards increase the frequency with which various kinds of responses are made, but a bit of candy given once every thousand responses is unlikely to have much influence on the behavior of a human adult.

Another somewhat more subtle problem is the validity of the experimental manipulation. In working with animals, for example, hours of deprivation of food or water has commonly served as the operational definition of drive induction, and there is now a good deal of evidence in support of this interpretation. But in some kinds of research, especially when novel methods are developed, evidence that a particular experimental manipulation is a valid operational definition of some theoretical variable may be very slim indeed. "Is the experimental threat in fact threatening?" "Is a proposed reinforcement in fact reinforcing?" This kind of question can be answered most confidently on the basis of previous research; therefore, if previous research has not demonstrated the validity or effectiveness of a particular experimental procedure, the safest way to evaluate the procedure is to do a preliminary pilot study using a small sample of subjects similar to those who will participate in the major research.

For further reference, see Carlsmith, Ellsworth, and Aronson, 1976, pp. 53-72.

SPECIFICITY OF METHODS AND OPERATIONAL DEFINITIONS

• *Is the procedure spelled out in enough concrete detail so that another trained researcher could repeat the research? Is there a clear, step-by-step description of the procedure?*

• *Is every variable defined operationally in terms of the measures or observations used to translate that variable into concrete steps of the research procedure?*

• *If there are alternatives in any phase of the procedure, are the methods of resolving these questions presented?*

Throughout the discussion of preceding points, research has been characterized in terms of a "line of inquiry." Implicit in this characterization is the assumption that the scientific enterprise involves some sort of interaction among those working on similar problems. We publish our studies; we read papers at professional meetings; we discuss our work with colleagues. All of this is part of the cumulative nature of scientific knowledge. Thus communication between researchers, involving the methods of one's investigation as well as the results and interpretation of findings, is an important part of the scientific enterprise.

Moreover, the process of spelling out a proposed method and tying down each phase of a research in concrete operational terms serves as a check on the investigator's own thinking. Sometimes a research seems to be conceptually meaningful and logically consistent as long as the researcher views it in abstract, theoretical terms; perhaps only when the study is made explicit in the step-by-step description of the procedures do the conceptual problems and logical inconsistencies become apparent.

Still another aspect of scientific inquiry is the stress on objectivity, which in one important sense means that other trained observers can repeat the procedures of a reported research to determine whether essentially the same results are obtained. Replicability, therefore, is an important characteristic of every research, for it is replication by others that affords a major way of establishing objectivity and testing the reliability of findings. Thus the methods and procedures of a research must be specified in enough concrete detail so that others can repeat the investigation.

CONTROLS IN THE RESEARCH PROCEDURE

• *Are the controls in the research procedure adequate, appropriate, and clearly specified?*

• *Are there any "incidental" features of the procedure that might bias the results and contaminate an interpretation of the data?*

• *Does the research plan take into account the subjects' possible expectations, sets, and interpretations of the research procedure?*

• *Has the investigator taken into account the possible influence of his or her wishes and expectations?*

An eventual aim in any line of scientific inquiry is to achieve knowledge of all the variables that influence a particular phenomenon. The history of inquiry in any field of research is typically characterized by increased control of relevant variables as the research moves from early descriptive studies to more refined experiments. In the psychology of learning, for example, the results of early studies were often confused by the effects of uncontrolled variables of which the experimenters were unaware. Gradually, as a consequence of numerous investigations, many of these variables were identified and controlled in subsequent research. The sensitivity of experiments in this field, or the accuracy with which predictions could be made and tested, was substantially increased over time. In designing research procedures, therefore, an investigator is responsible for identifying relevant variables on the basis of theory and previous research, and designing adequate controls for these variables.

As research progresses in any field, it is not uncommon for investigators to recognize that some aspects of their research procedures that heretofore had been considered "incidental," had, in fact, a significant influence on the results obtained. For example, if one is collecting data using a projective technique, it would be important to remember that the sex of the person administering the stimulus materials influences the responses that are elicited. The fact that a study is conducted in a school setting, in a laboratory, in a home, or in a local coffee shop can well be an important determinant of the results. The role of the investigator in relation to those who serve as subjects, whether he or she is teacher, friend, parent, or colleague, is also likely to make a difference in the data. In short, no aspect of the procedure can be considered "incidental" and irrelevant without careful consideration and, whenever possible, empirical investigation.

An important source of uncontrolled variance in some studies might be the subjects' implicit reactions during the research. Many people are likely to come into a study with some hunches or hypotheses about the purpose of the research, and they are also likely to develop some implicit interpretation of the procedures as they take part in them. Inasmuch as these hypotheses and interpretations influence behavior, they must be taken into account in planning research as well as in interpreting the results.

Another source of uncontrolled variance involves the researcher's own implicit wishes and expectations. The influence of these factors on the outcomes of research has been demonstrated dramatically in a series of investigations reported by Rosenthal and Rosnow (1969). Although the methods of scientific investigation must be objective and unbiased, it would be absurd in most cases to picture the scientist as a totally unbiased and objective machine. Of course the researcher is interested in the outcomes of research; he or she probably wouldn't be engaged in the activity unless he or she had some emotional involvement in what he or she was doing. Recognizing that investigators do have biases, many of the general principles of empirical investigation have been developed to help the investigator guard against his or her own wishes and expectations.

These "experimenter biases" inevitably affect a researcher's activities insofar as they influence the questions he or she investigates and the ways in which he or she formulates his research problems. *Explicit* theoretical biases can usually be identified readily in the report of any research and can be taken into account in interpreting the results. A more subtle problem, however, involves the investigator's *implicit* biases. He or she may not be aware of these biases, but they nevertheless influence behavior.

Perhaps the greatest opportunity for one's personal, implicit biases to operate *without awareness* is in designing and carrying out the procedures of a study. Certain procedures tend to elicit certain kinds of behaviors, and incidental features of the procedure, such as the emotional "tone" with which subjects are greeted, influence a subject's response to the total situation in which the research occurs. Subjects greeted warmly with a pleasant smile are likely to behave somewhat differently from those greeted neutrally or perhaps even with some subtle hostility. It is therefore most important for the investigator to examine his or her own wishes and expectations, to consider whether these have influenced the particular methods he or she has chosen, and to evaluate their possible effect on the ways in which the research procedures are implemented.

For further reference, see Carlsmith, Ellsworth, and Aronson, 1976, pp. 280–301.

OPPORTUNITIES FOR DISCOVERY

• *Is the procedure planned so that there is an opportunity for discovery? Should information other than that specified in the proposal be obtained?*

Before embarking on a major project in which a researcher will invest a great deal of time and energy, it is wise to scan the problem area with the aim of identifying information that might be obtained reasonably and economically in the course of the research, and that might eventually provide a useful basis for interpreting one's results, for relating one's findings to other studies, or perhaps for suggesting further approaches to the problem under investigation that may be potentially useful.

In conducting certain kinds of experiments, beginning researchers sometimes feel that talking to subjects is absolutely forbidden by the rules of scientific methodology. Indeed, this may be true during the experimental procedure itself, since, as indicated in a preceding section, anything that happens between the experimenter and the subject may influence the results of a study. But in some investigations, a brief postexperimental interview of the subjects might provide a useful source of information, not to test specific hypotheses, but rather, to provide leads for further research. Scientific investigators, like everyone else, are limited by their own sets and expectations, their own perceptual and cognitive habits. Discovery often means breaking these sets, these habitual ways of perceiving and thinking, and perhaps no technique for breaking sets about one's own work is more effective than talking to the subjects who have participated in one's research.

Of course one cannot plan discoveries, but the research method can be planned so that there is at least the opportunity for discovery. The researcher above all is an observer, and although much of research methodology is designed to focus observations under carefully controlled conditions, a well-planned study also permits the investigator to observe phenomena that might lead to new questions, novel hunches, and further hypotheses about the problems that are under investigation.

APPROPRIATENESS OF EXPERIMENTAL DESIGN

• *Has the researcher chosen the most efficient and effective experimental design—the design that will provide, within the practical limits of his or her investigation, the fullest answer to the questions posed or the most adequate test of the hypotheses presented?*

To a certain extent, the kind of information obtained in any research is determined by the overall strategy of investigation. Natural observation leads to broad descriptions of various phenomena, the identification of potentially important parameters and processes, the formulation of possibly significant questions. Correlational methods lead to more precise descriptions of a more limited range of phenomena in terms of the pattern of relationships found among the variables considered. The strategy of experimental manipulation leads to the most precise, typically the most controlled and narrowly focused investigation of particular relations among a few variables.

But within each of these broad strategic approaches there are a variety of tactics that might be used, and these tactics are reflected in the experimental design of a study. For example, using a correlational strategy, an investigator might choose to compare subjects who fall at the extremes of some dimension, such as psychological adjustment, with the aim of identifying gross differences between sharply contrasting groups. Within the practical limits in which a researcher is working, and in terms of the knowledge available at any given time, this design may be the most feasible and practical choice. But if one studies only subjects at the extremes of a distribution, certain nonlinear relations between variables cannot be determined. As knowledge about the various aspects of human behavior accumulates, however, the existence of nonlinear relations among variables is becoming more and more apparent.

In the strategy of experimental manipulation, a wide variety of design tactics might be used. A simple design in which the independent variable is manipulated and the effects measured in terms of a single dependent variable may be the tactic of choice at any point in a line of inquiry. This design certainly has the virtue of straightforward simplicity and may be exactly what is called for in resolving some clearly focused problem.

But at the present time in most areas of social science and educational investigation, theory and research have not yet reached a level of sophistication that permits the formulation of significant questions that can be answered by the simple independent-dependent variable design. The vast majority of problems in psychological and educational research are much too complex to be dealt with meaningfully in terms of a simple relationship between two variables. In most areas, we simply do not know enough to pinpoint a crucial relationship that warrants investigation without considering the effects of other variables. Almost all behavior is multidetermined, and any experimental manipulation is likely to have a variety of effects as a function of more than one variable. Thus, a large number of various experimental designs have been developed to deal with multivariate problems and should be used in most investigations. These take into account problems such as the order of experimental treatments, initial baseline of performance, the effects of repeated measurements, the use of correlated measures, and the interaction effects of several variables. Certainly none of these more complex designs should be used merely for the sake of pseudosophisticated complexity; this is a luxury few researchers can afford. Reasonable simplicity of design is a highly desirable characteristic of all research, but in most instances an experimental design providing for a multivariate analysis of the data is likely to be most useful and appropriate.

For further reference, see Kerlinger, 1973, pp. 300–347.

RELIABILITY AND PRECISION OF MEASUREMENT

• *What is the evidence in support of the reliability of every set of observations or measures used in the research?*

• *If reliability has not been established in previous research, how will it be evaluated in the proposed study?*

• *Is the researcher aware of any special problems of reliability that might be involved in the proposed research?*

• *Is the precision of the measurement procedures consistent with the intent of the research?*

Problems of reliability, in terms of both internal consistency and stability over time, have probably received most attention from those working in the psychometric areas of psychology. Every test constructor recognizes that part of his task in developing a measuring instrument is to establish its reliability, and a variety of techniques have been developed to deal with this general problem. But more recently we have come to appreciate the significance of this problem for all research, not only that area of research that deals with test construction.

Consider, for example, a typical study in the area of child development concerned with the relation between certain child rearing techniques and aggressiveness of children. Assume that a child's aggressiveness will be evaluated by judges who observe the child and rate his or her behavior on a series of scales, each of which is designed to reflect aggressiveness. In this case, the investigator is confronted by three somewhat different issues of reliability. First, the reliability of judges must be evaluated in terms of agreement among judges who observe the same behavior. Then, the internal consistency of the several scales designed to measure aggressiveness must be determined. Finally, the stability of the child's aggressiveness over time and different situations must be investigated. Thus, considering only a single variable in this study, one can readily appreciate the importance of reliability of measurement from several different points of view.

Each kind of research presents its own special problems in evaluating reliability, and every researcher must be familiar with the problems involved in his or her particular line of inquiry. If these problems are neglected, it is likely that the line of inquiry will be confused by inconsistent results. For example, unreliable measures have probably contributed a good deal to the difficulties encountered in research investigating changes in self concept. If a measure such as the discrepancy between a subject's self concept and his or her ideal self concept were used to evaluate change over time, the estimate of change in this discrepancy from one time to another would involve a difference of difference measures. This raises a special problem in reliability, for the reliability of a difference score tends to be lower than the reliability of each measure involved in obtaining the difference. In this case, the step-down in reliability is likely to be of considerable importance because the final estimate of change in self concept depends upon a second-order difference score. To be at all meaningful, one would have to begin this chain of difference scores with highly reliable measures; otherwise, by the second order of differences required by the research, the reliability would probably be too low to warrant serious consideration as a research measure.

This illustrates only one of many possible problems in reliability that an investigator might face. Although reliability of measurement is an important issue in every research, it becomes a crucial problem in the event null results are obtained, because one factor that may account for null results is the use of unreliable measures. Thus, a researcher would be forced to conclude that the research did not test the hypothesis he or she started with or investigate the question that initiated the research. The study, then, could hardly be considered a defensible investigation, and it would seem prudent to consider issues of reliability at the outset, rather than after the data have been collected.

One aspect of the general problem of reliability concerns the precision of measurement. As the researcher considers the reliability of the measures he or she plans to use, he or she must also evaluate the precision of the measures in light of the aims of the research. On the one hand, small, subtle differences cannot be measured with gross techniques of observation; on the other hand, needless time, money, and energy might be expended on developing an extremely refined measure to tap large and obvious differences. In most areas of psychological and educational research, our problem is hardly too much precision, but rather, too few instruments that provide anything but fairly rough approximations of the variables in which we are interested. In fact, research in some areas may be blocked because adequate measurement procedures have not yet been developed, and, in all areas of inquiry, significant advances often depend upon adequate refinement of the measures used.

For further reference see Anastasi, 1976, pp. 104-133; Thorndike and Hagen, 1977, pp. 73-101.

VALIDITY AND CHOICE OF MEASURES

• *What is the evidence of validity of every measure used? If the measure has been used in previous work, what is the evidence of validity in the literature? If the measure is developed for this specific research, what evidence of validity will be obtained?*

• *Are there other measures that might better be used?*

Problems of validity, of course, have been a central concern of a good deal of theory and research, and a number of extremely useful guides for an examination of this general problem have been published. If the research proposal is faulty in respect to this issue, perhaps the most useful step might be to review one of these references. However, there is a broader problem involved in the style of research in the behavioral and social sciences that warrants some attention in evaluating a proposal for new research. This style might be characterized as an anarchy of measurement.

Every researcher feels free to select or devise his or her own measures, and this freedom clearly is an important requisite of the overall research enterprise. Significant advances in any field would undoubtedly soon disappear if some group could, and in fact did, legislate the specific measures to be used in every research. At the heart of the research enterprise is the responsible freedom of the researcher.

But the emphasis in this concept must be equally on responsibility and freedom. In respect to problems of measurement, this means a certain responsibility to others engaged in the same general line of inquiry. The researcher is responsible for relating his or her particular study to other work in the field, not only conceptually, but also methodologically. Specifically, this means that if every researcher uses a different measure to define the same theoretical or conceptual variable, the likelihood that the findings of various researchers can be viewed cumulatively is sharply decreased.

In psychology at the present time, this anarchy of measurement seems to be characteristic of several areas of investigation. Consider, for example, the research literature dealing with impulse control, a variable of some theoretical importance from several points of view. A review of this literature indicates that at least a dozen different measures have been used by researchers, each presumably measuring the same variable. But a study following this review of the literature revealed that in one sample, at least, the correlations among a number of these measures were essentially zero (Robin, 1966). No wonder, then, that research results in this area tend to be inconsistent and even contradictory.

This is not a plea for some central legislation of measurement techniques, but in planning a new research there is no need to develop a new measure simply as a virtuoso display of the researcher's creativity. Of course some researches may require the development of new measures, and this usually represents a major effort in itself. But in many studies, previously developed measures can and should be used. This acts to relieve the investigator of considerable preliminary work and also acts to increase the likelihood of continuity from one study to another.

For further reference, see Anastasi, 1976, pp. 134-161; Thorndike and Hagen, 1977, pp. 56-73.

APPROPRIATENESS OF STATISTICAL DESCRIPTION AND ANALYSIS

• *Is an appropriate statistical description and analysis of the results made explicit?*

• *When appropriate, are alternative ways of analyzing the data suggested?*

• *Are the assumptions involved in the statistical analysis recognized, and are the data likely to meet these assumptions? Is the investigator aware of possible problems in the statistical analysis?*

• *At each step in the proposal, as in determining the size of the sample, for instance, or in constructing the research design, have the appropriate statistical considerations been made?*

Statistics are used to describe data and to establish a quantitative basis for making inferences or generalizations from the results of a study. To a certain extent, the descriptive statistics a researcher uses—mean, standard deviation, or range—reflect conventions designed to aid in thinking about data. For example, the individual scores of 30 subjects on a learning task can be described by a measure of central tendency, such as the mean, and a measure of variability, such as the standard deviation. Thus, instead of the 30 individual scores, the investigator can more conveniently and easily view the results in terms of only two numbers that describe the distribution of scores he or she has obtained.

These kinds of descriptive quantitative techniques are useful intellectual devices that can help us think about extremely complex phenomena. They are, in a sense, like shorthand summaries of a great deal of information, but of course they also involve a certain loss of information. Using the mean and standard deviation, for instance, two aspects of a distribution of scores are described, but the score of any single individual cannot be determined. Thus, any descriptive technique can obscure, as well as clarify, the results of an investigation. It is therefore important for the investigator to choose appropriate descriptive statistics, basing his or her choice on the purpose of the research and the nature of the data obtained.

Having described the data, the investigator is then concerned with generalizing from the results. Rarely is he or she interested only in the particular sample studied; the aim is to determine whether it is reasonable to generalize the findings to the population he or she has sampled. For this purpose, a wide variety of inferential statistics have been devised, each designed to answer specific questions with certain kinds of data. In choosing an inferential statistic, the investigator must keep a number of considerations in mind. For example, does a particular statistical test provide a clearcut basis for answering the research question posed? Do the data meet the assumptions involved in a specific statistical analysis? What is the power of each of several possible statistical tests?

At the beginning of a research, an investigator may not be able to predict with confidence that certain assumptions underlying a statistical test will be satisfied by the data, and sometimes a number of different statistical analyses are possible. The choice may well depend upon an initial descriptive treatment of the data. Nevertheless, recognizing that final decisions about the choice of a specific statistic sometimes cannot be made until after the data are obtained and described, it is most important that the logic of the statistical analysis be incorporated within the logic of the overall plan of research.

For further reference, see Nunnally, 1975, pp. 63-83, 177-204.

INTERPRETATION OF RESULTS

• *Can various kinds of possible results be interpreted meaningfully? Can positive findings be integrated with previous research and theory? Can negative or null results be interpreted in a way that contributes to knowledge in the field? Would negative or null results make a difference in the area of investigation, in theory or practice?*

Every well-designed and well-executed research leads to meaningful results. In some instances, these results might contradict the investigator's initial expectations or wishes, and these studies may sometimes be the most important kinds of research. A researcher may begin with the utmost faith in the superiority of a particular technique in achieving a desired result; indeed, he or she may design the investigation in the spirit of a demonstration of the superiority of the chosen technique. But regardless of whether the study supports or contradicts the investigator's own faith, hunches, or beliefs, the important criterion for evaluating the results of a study is the degree to which it contributes knowledge to a given line of inquiry.

A special problem for some researchers is finding null results, no consistent differences, and no statistically significant correlations, F ratios, or t values. Perhaps this is because success in research has come to be identified with statistical significance. At any rate, regardless of the basis for this prejudice, the scientific quality of a research does not necessarily depend on whether statistically significant differences are found.

Many researchers begin their work with a conviction that their hypothesis will be supported, and they are usually much better prepared to interpret positive results than they are null results. At the outset in planning a research proposal, therefore, the researcher is well advised to consider the variety of possible results he or she might obtain, and to include in planning the avenues of interpretation he or she might take in the event the initial faith is not supported. In general, the plausibility of a hypothesis, the *a priori* probability of predicted outcome, must be sufficiently high so that negative or null results are of scientific interest, and the research must be designed so that such results are interpretable.

For further reference, see Kerlinger, 1973, pp. 134-156.

THE LANGUAGE OF RESEARCH:
DEFINITIONS AND APPLICATIONS

Analysis of Variance

A statistical test for determining whether there are significant differences among the means of several groups or among several experimental treatments. *Example:* A researcher investigates possible differences in learning associated with three different teaching methods and students in three groups differing in intellectual ability (e.g., very bright, below normal). An analysis of variance would permit an evaluation of the statistical significance of differences in learning scores obtained for the three different methods, for the three different groups of students, and whether there is a consistent relationship between teaching methods and intelligence of the students. (See *Interaction*)

Artifacts

Factors the researcher is probably unaware of, and thus does not control adequately, but that influence the results obtained. *Example:* A researcher investigates the relation between body build and personality. In the research procedure, ratings are made of both body build and personality. Any relationship he finds between these factors may be artifactual; that is, the results may be due to the researcher's own beliefs about body build and personality, and, without being aware of it, these beliefs may very well have influenced the ratings.

Bias

A variable that influences results in some systematic way. *Example:* A potentially important source of bias is the researcher's beliefs or expectations. Without being aware of it, an experimenter may influence the ways in which subjects behave by very subtle cues. For instance, the experimenter might smile whenever a subject behaves in a way that fits the experimenter's hypothesis, or the experimenter might turn away when a subject behaves in a way that doesn't fit the hypothesis. Another common source of potential bias is the selection of subjects. In studying the effects of two different teaching methods, an experimenter might assign relatively brighter subjects to one group and less bright subjects to the other group. Thus, any difference obtained could not be ascribed to the difference in methods, since the bias in selecting subjects has not been controlled. (See *Control*)

Chi Square

A statistical technique for determining whether the distributions of frequencies for any event are different either from chance or from a theoretically expected distribution. This statistic can be used with a wide variety of research data. *Example:* A researcher wants to know whether men and women voted differently on a particular school bond issue. In a sample of men, the researcher discovers that 69 voted *Yes* and 23 voted *No*; in a sample of women, the researcher discovers that 54 voted *Yes* and 41 voted *No*. To evaluate these results statistically, a chi-square test could be computed to determine the likelihood that the distributions of *Yes* and *No* obtained for men and women could have occurred by chance.

Concurrent Validity

The degree to which test results are related to other relevant measures taken at approximately the same time as the test. *Example:* A researcher develops a test to measure aggressiveness in interpersonal relations. To evaluate the concurrent validity of this measure, scores on this test are compared with ratings of aggressive behavior obtained from people who observe the subjects in their day-to-day interactions with others. Another researcher develops a measure of academic achievement motivation. The concurrent validity of this measure is evaluated by comparing scores on this test with teachers' and fellow students' ratings of how hard each person works to achieve in school.

Construct Validity

The degree to which a test measures the construct it is supposed to measure. Construct validity is evaluated by the opinion of experts in the area covered by the test, and by the relationship of the test in question with measures of other relevant constructs. *Example:* A researcher develops a measure of test anxiety. One source of information about the construct validity of this measure is the judgment of other people who have had a good deal of experience studying test anxiety. This is the kind of evidence a researcher would be likely to collect before investing a large amount of time and energy in using this measure in the research. Essentially, he or she would ask others who are considered experts in the field whether they believe this test is likely to measure test anxiety. In addition, the researcher would also evaluate the construct validity of the measure by determining whether it is related to measures of other constructs one would reasonably expect it to be related to. In this instance, one would expect a measure of test anxiety to be related to a measure of general school adjustment. That is, a student whose score on the particular measure shows high test anxiety would be expected to score relatively low on a measure of general school adjustment, assuming that an already validated measure of general school adjustment is available. If the researcher found that the measure of test anxiety was unrelated to a measure of general school adjustment, the construct validity of the measure would be questioned.

Content Analysis

Classifying the information contained in any communication according to a defined set of categories and following explicit rules of coding. *Example:* A researcher wishes to investigate whether psychology is favorably presented in various mass media. A sample of magazines published on one given day is selected. The researcher also explicitly defines three categories: (1) favorable statements about psychology, (2) unfavorable statements about psychology, and (3) neutral statements about psychology. After carefully defining each category, the investigator reads the magazines, identifies the relevant statements, and classifies each statement according to his or her rules for coding. Frequencies of statements in each of the three categories can be tabulated, and, on the basis of this content analysis, the investigator could come to some conclusion about the way psychology is presented in the magazines sampled.

Content Validity

The degree to which a measure involves or accurately reflects the actual content of the variable measured. Content validity is evaluated by systematically comparing the content of the test to the measurement objectives. *Example:* As part of a research program evaluating student achievement in a school system, a test of English grammar is developed. The content validity of this test depends upon the degree to which it deals with significant information about English grammar. If the test is made up largely of items that are trivial in learning English grammar, it would have relatively low content validity. But if the test accurately covers the range of important facts and ideas a student should know about English grammar, its content validity would be relatively high.

Control Group

Strictly speaking, this term refers only to experimental investigations involving the manipulation of one or more variables. Thus, the experimenter might manipulate the critical variable with one group, and compare the results obtained for this group with those of a control group with whom he did not manipulate the particular variable. In practice, the term "control group" is sometimes used in nonexperimental research to refer to the group who are not "special" in any way relevant to the major focus of the research. This group typically serves as the basis for comparison with the subjects who are of primary interest in the research. *Example:* A researcher comparing reaction times of schizophrenic patients and a sample of psychologically normal people might refer to this latter group as the "control group." In a sense, the control group provides the baseline data against which the results for the experimental group (or group of special interest) are compared. *Example:* A researcher is investigating the effects of hunger on word associations. All subjects participate in the experiment between 9:30 and 11 in the morning, but the subjects in the experimental group have been deprived of food for 24 hours whereas subjects in the control group have eaten on a normal schedule. Thus, the experimenter can interpret possible differences in word associations as a function of food deprivation or hunger.

Controls

When investigating possible relationships among variables, the researcher wants to be confident that the relationships observed reflect the actual facts, rather than some bias, contamination, or mistake in the research procedures. This is achieved by various techniques of control, including, for example, random sampling of subjects, careful design of experimental methods to ensure that extraneous or uncontrolled variables don't influence the results, measurement of possibly related variables, various statistical procedures, etc. In fact, much of what is involved in learning to do research may be thought of in terms of learning to achieve appropriate controls in investigation. *Example:* A researcher wants to compare the effectiveness of two different ways of teaching American history. Before beginning the research, the investigator knows that student learning is affected by the student's interest in a particular topic. Therefore, he or she knows that, in one way or another, it will be necessary to control for student interest in the area of American history involved in the research. One way this control might be achieved is by measuring student interest, and setting up matched pairs of students, with the students in each pair showing the same ("matched") level of interest. Then, the experimenter would randomly assign one student in each pair to Method A and the other one to Method B. Thus, differences in student interest in the study would be controlled for. This method may also be used for controlling other factors that previous experience, theory, and research suggest are relevant to the study. This is only one way of achieving control; the particular kind of controls a researcher uses depends upon the research strategy, previous knowledge in the area of research, the specific nature of the research problem, and the setting in which the investigator works.

Correlation

A statistical technique for evaluating the degree to which variables vary together. If two variables increase and decrease together, the correlation is positive; if one variable increases when the other decreases, and vice versa, the correlation is negative. A correlation of $+1.00$ indicates a perfect, one-to-one relationship; as one variable decreases, the other decreases proportionately. A correlation of -1.00 indicates a perfect inverse relationship; as one variable increases, the other decreases proportionately, and as one variable decreases, the other increases proportionately. A correlation of 0.00 indicates that the two variables are independent of each other; that is, there is no systematic relationship between the variables. A commonly used correlation statistic is the Pearson product moment correlation coefficient (usually abbreviated as r). Another statistic, used with ranked data, is the rank order correlation coefficient (called rho). Multiple correlations (abbreviated as R) are computed to evaluate the relationships among several variables. *Example:* Suppose a researcher is interested in the relationship between reading ability and mathematical ability. He or she would measure each of these abilities and compute a correlation coefficient to determine the degree to which these two abilities covary.

Correlational Design

A research strategy designed to investigate how two or more variables covary. In contrast to an experimental design, the researchers using a correlational model do not manipulate any of the variables involved. They merely measure each variable as it occurs naturally, and then study the relationships among the variables measured. A correlational design of research should not be confused with a correlation statistic; other statistics may also be used. *Example:* Suppose a researcher is interested in the relation between years of teaching experience and the kinds of questions a teacher asks when teaching. For each teacher in the sample, two kinds of information are obtained: (1) years of teaching experience, and (2) the kinds of questions the teacher asks. The investigator would then divide the sample of teachers into subgroups on the basis of years of experience (e.g., 0-5, 6-10, more than 10), and categorize the kinds of questions teachers in each subgroup asked. The analysis of data would focus on whether years of teaching experience was systematically associated with the pattern of questions the teachers asked.

Cross Validation

A research strategy in which relationships found in one set of data are investigated in another set of data to determine whether the same relationships hold. This strategy is used when researchers are unable to formulate specific questions or hypotheses on the basis of theory or previous research. *Example:* A researcher wants to identify characteristics that distinguish effective from ineffective teachers. He or she would measure teaching effectiveness of a large number of teachers and select the 100 most effective and 100 least effective teachers. Then, information about a wide range of characteristics would be collected from all 200 teachers. If the researcher chose to follow a cross-validation strategy with these data, he or she would randomly select 50 of the 100 most effective teachers and 50 of the 100 least effective teachers. On the basis of these data, it would be possible to determine which of the many characteristics that had been measured differentiated the sample of 50 most effective from the sample of 50 least effective teachers.

Suppose that the investigator had measured 25 characteristics, and of these, five showed statistically significant differences on the first half of the data. These five characteristics would be treated as hypotheses and the investigator could cross-validate the findings with the data for the remaining subjects. That is, the researcher would analyze the data for the 50 most effective and 50 least effective teachers who were not selected in the first step of the analysis. The aim in this step would be to determine whether the statistically significant differences for the 5 characteristics obtained in the first part of the analysis held up with the second half of the data. If the results are consistent for the two halves of the data, confidence in the findings would be substantially enhanced.

Deduction

Reasoning from universal to the individual cases, from the general to the particular, or from a set of premises to their logical conclusion. *Example:* One might begin with the proposition that punishment evokes an unpleasant emotional state in the person who is punished. People generally try to avoid feeling unpleasant and thus try to avoid situations in which they anticipate punishment. Therefore, if students are frequently punished by a particular teacher, when they are given freedom of choice, they will tend to avoid that teacher.

Degrees of Freedom

A phrase used in tests of statistical inference, referring to the number of statistically independent observations. It is used to make adjustments in certain statistical tests. *Example:* Suppose the mean of a sample of 10 scores is 100. This means that the sum of the 10 scores is 1000, since the mean is the sum of scores divided by the number of scores (in other words, the arithmetic average). The degrees of freedom for the mean is $10 - 1$, or 9. If the sum of the 10 scores must be 1000, nine of the scores are "free" to vary, but then the tenth one would be fixed in order to make a total of 1000. If the first nine scores added up to 950, the tenth score would have to be 50. Thus, there are 9 degrees of freedom.

Dependent Variable

Primarily used in referring to variables involved in experimental studies. In the simplest experimental design, the experimenter manipulates one variable and measures the effect of that manipulation on a second variable. This second variable is the dependent variable. In a sense, one might think of an experiment as a way of determining whether this second variable is in fact "dependent" on the variable manipulated by the experimenter. When used in discussing nonexperimental research, it refers to the variable that theory specifies as the effect or consequence of some other variable or variables. *Example:* An experimenter wishes to study the effect of different amounts of reward on rate of learning in children. For one group, the researcher rewards correct responses with one cent; for a second group, he or she rewards correct response with five cents. Everything else is equated for the two groups. Then, the investigator measures the rate of learning to determine whether there is a difference between the group rewarded with one cent and the group rewarded with five cents. In this case, rate of learning is the dependent variable. The experiment is designed to determine whether rate of learning is "dependent" on amount of reward.

In more complex experiments, of course, there may be more than one dependent variable, but the same logic holds in defining dependent variables regardless of the complexity of the experiment.

Descriptive Statistics

A variety of techniques used to describe quantitatively in summary form the data obtained in a research. Descriptive statistics presented in a research report typically include some measure of central tendency and some measure of variability. *Example:* The central tendency of a distribution of scores may be described by the mean, the median, or the mode. The variability of this distribution of scores may be described by the variance, the standard deviation, or the range. There are many different ways of describing data statistically, and one of the important early steps in planning any statistical analysis is deciding upon the descriptive statistics that will be most useful for the purposes of the particular research.

Double-blind Experiment

An experimental procedure in which neither the subject nor the experimenter knows the specific experimental treatment administered to a given subject until after the data are collected. This procedure is used to guard against possible biases an experimenter might introduce into the data collection process without being aware of these biases. *Example:* An experimenter might believe that a certain drug was very effective in reducing anxiety. In testing the effectiveness of this drug by comparing the anxiety level of people who received the drug with those who did not receive the drug, the experimenter's bias, without awareness, might influence the way he or she relates to people in the two groups and the observations made about their anxiety. In addition, if the subjects themselves knew whether they were receiving the drug, they might be influenced merely by the subtle suggestion or expectation that there will be an effect. Therefore, the experimenter would use a procedure in which both the researcher and the subjects did not know which ones had received the drug until after the data were collected. (See *Placebo*)

Empirical

Refers to methods of investigation based on observations. Whenever observational methods are used to collect data in a research, the study is empirical. *Example:* Consider the question, "Is it raining?". An empirical method to answer this question would be to go outside and look. A nonempirical method would be to debate about this question, without collecting any observational evidence.

Experiment

A strategy of investigation in which the researcher systematically manipulates one or more variables and measures the effect of this manipulation on other variables. *Example:* What is the effect of room temperature on classroom learning? Keeping all other conditions the same, the researcher systematically varies the temperature of classrooms and measures the effect in terms of learning.

Extreme Group Design

A research design involving the comparison of subjects at the two extremes of a distribution. Although this design is sometimes used because of practical considerations, such as the expense of collecting data for each subject, it should be used with caution because of potentially important information that might be missed when only extreme groups are studied. *Example:* Researchers want to investigate the relationship between test anxiety and performance on a given test. They measure the test anxiety of 250 students, and, using an extreme group design, compare the performance of the 25 students showing highest test anxiety with the performance of the 25 students showing lowest test anxiety. This design is efficient and economical if the relationship between the two variables is linear. Research following this design will miss crucial information if the relationship is not linear, however. For instance, if students with moderate test anxiety perform better than those with either high or low anxiety, an extreme group design will miss this information.

F Ratio

The quotient of one variance divided by another variance, sometimes referred to as an *F Test*. The *F* ratio is the end product of an analysis of variance and indicates the probability that the results obtained are due to chance. Probability levels are given in tables of the *F* distribution.

Factor Analysis

A method based on the correlations among a set of variables, providing a statistical basis for identifying the factors underlying individual differences along a number of dimensions. *Example:* A researcher obtains ratings from hospitalized patients on 25 scales designed to reflect various aspects of their experiences of suffering. As a first step, the intercorrelations among these scales are computed, and by factor analysis of these intercorrelations the researcher identifies two factors that account for most of the variation on these 25 scales. These two factors might be physical pain and psychological distress.

Factorial Design

A research designed to investigate simultaneously the effects of various levels of two or more variables on a third variable. *Example:* A researcher wishes to study the effect of different kinds of reward (verbal praise versus money) and socioeconomic class of students (low versus middle) on learning. Following a factorial design, four groups of Ss might be formed: (1) lower-class students receiving verbal praise; (2) lower-class students receiving money reward; (3) middle-class students receiving verbal praise; and (4) middle-class students receiving money reward. By analysis of variance of the learning scores shown in these four groups, the researcher could simultaneously evaluate the effect of type of reward, socioeconomic class of student, and the interaction between type of reward and socioeconomic class. The factorial design for this study can be diagrammed as follows:

		Reward	
		Verbal Praise	Money
Social Class	Lower-Class		
	Middle-Class		

(See *Interaction*)

Frequency Distribution

A technique for describing a set of observations. Essentially, the range of observations is divided into scores or categories, and the frequency of each score or each category is tabulated. The summary of this tabulation is a frequency distribution. *Example:* Suppose scores on a test were 80, 90, or 100. Ten people got 80; fifteen people got 90; and twelve people got 100. The frequency distribution would be:

Score	Frequency
80	10
90	15
100	12

Hawthorne Effect

A more or less temporary change obtained simply as a result of introducing something new into a situation. The term derives from an early
study of industrial productivity done at an electric company in Hawthorne,
Illinois. *Example:* A researcher investigates the effect of various conditions
on amount of work students do in a classroom. The investigator increases
lighting, and for a day or two, students work more. Soft background music
is introduced, and for a day or two, students work more. But none of the
effects lasts very long. The changes the researcher observes probably reflect
the Hawthorne Effect of merely introducing something new into the
classrooms.

Hypothesis

A researcher's conjecture about the relationship of two or more variables. Hypotheses are statements predicting results prior to conducting a
research. *Examples:* Stress interferes with learning. Reading ability is
positively related to mathematical ability. Speech problems are more fre-
quent in boys than in girls.

Idiographic Research

Study of an individual, unique case or event. *Example:* A group of
researchers wishes to study the relationship between a teacher's mood and
his or her classroom behavior. They choose to study a single teacher inten-
sively over time. Each weekday for a month, they obtain measures of the
mood of a particular teacher and also observe and record that teacher's
behavior in class. The results of this study will permit the researchers to
draw conclusions about the teacher observed. They will also provide a
basis for formulating hypotheses about the relationship of mood and
classroom behavior for other teachers.

Independent Variable

Used primarily in referring to variables in experimental studies. Refers
to the variable or variables in the research manipulated by the experimenter. When used in discussing nonexperimental research, it refers to the
variable that is the presumed cause or antecedent condition of another
variable considered in the research. *Example:* A researcher wishes to investigate the relationship between size of type and speed of oral reading.
The independent variable is size of type, and the experimenter manipulates

his variable by preparing reading materials with the same content, but varying in size of type. The experimenter then presents the material in different sizes of type to randomly selected samples and measures speed of oral reading, the dependent variable.

Indirect Assessment

Measurement techniques in which the purpose of the measure is disguised. *Examples:* The Thematic Apperception Test (TAT) consists of a series of pictures about which the person is asked to tell stories. It is sometimes presented as a test of imagination, although the actual purpose is to learn about the person's personality. Another indirect assessment technique involves "error choices." The measure is presented as a test of information, but all the choices for particular items are factually wrong. If a person consistently chooses answers in one direction, this presumably reflects his attitude about the topic rather than his knowledge. Suppose the real purpose of the research is to study attitudes toward men and women. Each item is presented as an information test with one choice favorable to men and the other choice favorable to women. For instance, one item might be: Research has shown that: (a) women are smarter than men; (b) men are smarter than women. If we consistently choose answers favorable to one sex or the other, this presumably reflects our attitudes toward men or women.

Induction

Reasoning from particulars to general statements, from individual instances to the universal, from a part to the whole. *Example:* Suppose we observe a random sample of classrooms in a given school, and in each of the classrooms we note a very high level of student participation. On the basis of induction, we might expect all, or at least most, of the other classes in the school to be characterized by a high level of student participation.

Interaction

Generally refers to the effects of two variables on each other. Commonly used by researchers to refer specifically to statistical interaction in which the effect of one variable varies as a function of another variable. This "interaction effect" may be evaluated by analysis of variance or covariance techniques. *Example:* Suppose researchers are interested in children's perceptions of their own power to make important decisions. They might find that the perceptions of boys differ from those of girls, but they might also find that the difference between boys and girls is a function of

rural-urban locales. In the rural sample, boys see themselves as more power-
ful than girls do. Thus, girls differ from boys in perceptions of their own
power, but the nature or direction of this difference depends upon the locale
of the children. The difference found in one locale is exactly opposite from
what was found in the other locale. In statistical terms, there is an interaction between sex of the child and locale.

Interval Scale

A scale in which the categories are mutually exclusive and can be ordered in terms of the amount of a given characteristic. In addition, equal
differences in scale points reflect equal differences in amount of the characteristic. For instance, the difference represented by scale points 7 and 5 is
equal to the difference represented by scale points 3 and 1. *Example:* Measuring temperature by a thermometer provides an interval scale. Although
most rating scales used in psychological and educational research are ordinal scales rather than interval scales, they are often treated statistically as if
they were interval scales. This seems to be a useful "error" in statistical
analysis, and although this "error" is permitted by virtue of current conventions in research, an investigator should be aware of the nature of the
scales he uses and whether the assumption of approximately interval scale
units is reasonable for his particular measures.

Item Analysis

Procedures for selecting items to improve validity and reliability of a
test. Various techniques of item analysis are concerned with difficulty level
and discriminative value of an item. The optimum level and range of difficulty depend upon the purpose of the test. The discriminative value of an
item refers to the degree that item reflects individual differences in the
characteristic the test is designed to measure. *Example:* We wish to develop
a test of health knowledge for high school students. Our first task is to
construct a large number of items and administer them to a sample of students. On the basis of these data, we eliminate items that are too easy (e.g.,
passed by everyone) or too hard (e.g., failed by everyone). We also eliminate items that fail to differentiate students who have studied health for at
least one year and students who have never studied health.

Main Effects

Refers to differences obtained in relation to a single variable in an
analysis of variance or covariance. *Example:* The research is designed to
investigate the relationship of age (30-35 versus 15-20) and sex (male

versus female) on pain threshold. Four groups are involved: older females, older males, younger females, and younger males. An analysis of variance of the pain threshold measures would evaluate two main effects: (1) younger versus older subjects, and (2) male versus female subjects. It would also evaluate the interaction effect, in terms of differences in one variable (such as age) as a function of the other variable (sex). (See *Interaction*)

Matched Groups

To make sure that the effect measured in an experiment is due to the experimental manipulation, the researcher must control all other potentially relevant variables. One way to achieve this is by matching subjects assigned to the various groups in the study. Thus, if people of different ages might respond differently to the experimental manipulation, the experimenter could control for age by pairing individuals on the basis of age. Assuming two groups are involved in the study, if a 16-year-old is assigned to one group, another 16-year-old would be assigned to the other group. The two groups, then, would be matched for age. *Example:* A research compares the effects on reading comprehension of two different methods of teaching reading. Initial reading ability is likely to be an important factor, so the experimenter wishes to control this variable in forming the groups taught by the two different teaching methods. Before the experiment begins, a test of reading ability is administered. Then, in assigning subjects to the two groups, if a subject with high reading ability is assigned to one group, a subject of equal ability is assigned to the other group. Matching is used in conjunction with randomization. In this study, for instance, after two subjects with equal reading ability have been matched, which of the two subjects is assigned to a particular experimental group is determined on a random basis, such as flipping a coin.

Mean

The arithmetic average of a set of observations, measures, or scores; probably the most frequently used measure of the central tendency of a distribution. *Example:* Scores obtained by seven people on a spelling test are: 70, 75, 75, 80, 85, 90, 95. The mean is computed by summing these scores (570) and dividing by the number of observations (7). The number, usually abbreviated as $\overline{X}$, is 81.43.

Median

The observation or score that divides the distribution in half. It is the point below which (and above which) 50 percent of the cases lie. A frequently-used measure of central tendency when the distribution of observations seems to be quite different from the bell-shaped normal curve. *Example:* Scores obtained by seven people on a spelling test are 70, 75, 75, 80, 85, 90, 95. The median score of this distribution is 80. (See the *mean* obtained for the same distribution of scores.)

Mode

A measure of central tendency. The observation or score that occurs most frequently in a distribution. When there are two scores that occur with equal frequency, a distribution is said to be *bimodal. Example:* Scores obtained by seven people on a spelling test are 70, 75, 75, 80, 85, 90, 95. The mode is 75, since this is the score that occurs most frequently in this distribution. (Compare the *mean, median,* and *mode* of this distribution. All are measures of central tendency.)

Naturalistic Observation

A strategy of research in which the investigator observes what happens in the natural world as systematically and objectively as possible. In contrast to other strategies, the researcher does not manipulate any variable (as in experimental research) or use more formal measures (as in correlational research). In fact, the researcher usually tries to use procedures that will minimize any effects his methods of observation might have on the natural environment. *Example:* A researcher wishes to study the ways people behave while waiting for their dental appointments. Using the strategy of naturalistic observation, the investigator sits in a dentist's reception room and records everything he observes while patients are waiting for their appointments. To make the observations easier and probably more reliable, the researcher could develop an observational guide specifying the kinds of behaviors to be recorded and the frequency with which these observations of each patient will be noted.

Nominal Scale

A scale in which the categories included in the scale are mutually exclusive and are not quantitatively ordered along any given dimension. The scale provides a simple categorization of observations. *Examples:* Patients in a hospital might be categorized on the basis of type of illness. Students in a school might be classified on the basis of religion. Both of these would be nominal scales. (See *Interval* and *Ordinal* scales)

Nomothetic Research

Research designed to investigate relationships that can be generalized to the population of people sampled in a given study. At the present time, this is by far the most common kind of research in psychology and education, in contrast to research that focuses on a single case. (See *Idiographic research*)

Nonparametric Statistics

Techniques of statistical inference that do not depend upon the assumption that the variables studied are distributed in any particular way in the population. The most frequently used inferential tests (e.g., *t*-tests, analysis of variance) are based on the assumption that the variable being studied is normally distributed in the population sampled. If the distribution of observations obtained for the sample differs a great deal from the normal, bell-shaped curve, a nonparametric statistic might be more appropriate than the more commonly used *t*-test or analysis of variances. Nonparametric tests include, for example, chi square, median test, sign test, and rank-sum test.

Normal Curve

A distribution that takes the form of a bell-shaped curve, with specific areas covered by the curve determined mathematically on the basis of the theory of probability. Values referring to areas under the curve are tabled in most statistics textbooks and are used to evaluate the probability of certain inferential statistics.

Norms

The average and variability of scores obtained by a representative sample at each age level, grade level, or other set of categories relevant to a test. By reference to the norms for a given test, the relative position of a particular score can be determined. *Example:* A 10-year-old child obtains a score of 39 on a vocabulary test. Is this score high or low for 10-year-olds? This question could be answered if norms are available for a representative sample of 10-year-olds on this test. For example, reference to the norms might indicate that a score of 39 is higher than 90 percent of 10-year-old children upon whom the norms are based. Thus, in this instance, 39 would be considered a high score.

Null Hypothesis

Used in tests of statistical inference. Specifically, refers to the hypothe sis that there is no difference between groups or no relationship between variables. Tests of statistical inference provide a basis for deciding whether to reject the null hypothesis. If the null hypothesis is rejected (e.g., the hypothesis that there is no difference between groups), the research hypoth esis is supported. In a research plan, the research hypothesis, *not* the null hypothesis, is presented. *Example:* The research hypothesis of a study is that 8-year-old girls can jump higher than 8-year-old boys. Data are col lected on a sample of boys and a sample of girls, and a *t*-test is used to evaluate the statistical significance of the difference in means observed for these two groups. The null hypothesis tested statistically is that girls and boys do not differ in how high they can jump. The *t*-test provides a statis tical basis for determining whether the null hypothesis can reasonably be rejected and the research hypothesis supported.

Objective

An observation is said to be objective when it is independent of pos sible biases or distortions associated with the perspective of a particular observer. Mechanical means of recording observations, assuming the ma chines are functioning properly, are objective because they are not influ enced by an observer. A multiple-choice test is said to be objective, in comparison to an essay test, because evaluation of a specific person's answers does not depend upon the judgment of a particular judge. Ratings are said to be objective when there is consistently high agreement among raters, indicating that the ratings are not influenced by the subjective biases of a particular rater.

One-Tailed Test

A statistical term referring to a basis for evaluating the probability of an inferential statistic. In most cases, the null hypothesis is tested: A is no different from B. This hypothesis will be rejected if A is much larger than B, or if B is much larger than A. This is a two-tailed test, since it considers possible differences at both ends of a theoretical distribution in which A is greater than B at one end, and B is greater than A at the other end. But suppose that the researcher makes a hypothesis specifying the direction of the difference (e.g., A is greater than B), and differences in the opposite direction (B is greater than A) are of no theoretical interest. Thus, only one end of the distribution is of concern, and a one-tailed test would be used.

Operational Definition

Defining a variable in terms of the procedures, operations, observaions, or tests used to measure that variable. *Example:* Arithmetic ability night be defined operationally by the score obtained on the arithmetic sub-est of the Metropolitan Achievement Test.

Ordinal Scale

A scale in which the categories are mutually exclusive and can be or-lered in terms of the amount of a given characteristic. The difference in amount represented by an interval in the scale is not known, however. For example, a scale rating of 2 means a greater amount of the characteristic than a rating of 1, but the size of this difference cannot be specified. *Example:* A researcher wishing to evaluate students' responses to a particular course uses a five-point scale running from (1) It's Terrible to (5) It's Great. A higher rating means a more positive (or less negative) evaluation, but the researcher cannot specify "how much more positive" a rating of 5 is than a rating of 4. Although many rating scales used in psychological and educational research are, strictly speaking, ordinal scales, they are frequently treated statistically as if they were interval scales. (See *Interval* and *Nominal* Scales)

Parameter

If a particular characteristic were measured for all cases in a population, any measure derived from these measures would be a parameter. Almost all research deals with samples or portions of a population. Thus, all cases in a population are not measured. Parameters, therefore, are estimated on the basis of measures obtained for the sample. *Example:* Suppose a population is defined as all the 12-year-old girls in School X. If the height of every 12-year-old girl in the school was measured, the average height would be a parameter. The standard deviation of these measures would also be a parameter.

Percentile

Indicates the percent of people in the sample who fell below a given score. *Example:* A person receives a raw score of 20 on a test of English grammar. Referring to the norms for this test, one finds that a score of 20 corresponds to the 35th percentile. This means that 35 percent of the people upon whom this test was standardized obtained scores below 20.

Pilot Study

Prior to conducting a large-scale research, it is usually wise to carry out a preliminary study, perhaps going through the entire procedure with a very small sample or going through those parts of the procedure with which the researcher is not familiar. Although pilot studies mean extra time at the beginning of a research, in the long run they often save a good deal of time, effort, and money by anticipating problems the researcher can deal with before embarking on a major study.

Placebo

Sometimes, people change simply because they think they are receiving some kind of treatment. Therefore, in evaluating the effects of a particular treatment, a researcher would also study a placebo control group in which the subjects are exposed to the same general procedures as the treatment group, but do not in fact receive the specific treatment being evaluated. *Example:* A researcher wishes to evaluate the effects of a new drug on feelings of tension. Half the subjects, randomly selected, would receive the new drug in pill form, and the other half would receive a placebo—that is, a pill that looks and tastes like the experimental drug, but actually consists of a physiologically inert substance.

Population

All of a set of individuals or objects having some common characteristics. Any subset of the population is a sample. *Example:* The population of human females in the world at the present time consists of all people who are female living at this moment. (See *Sample*)

Predictive Validity

The degree to which a measure predicts the future behavior it is designed to predict. *Example:* A researcher develops a measure of nursing aptitude that is designed to predict how well a student will do in nursing school. To investigate the predictive validity of the measure, the investigator administers the test before students begin their nursing training. Then, one year later, the researcher obtains evaluations of the performance of each student in nursing school and compares these evaluations with the scores on the test of nursing aptitude.

Projective Technique

The way in which a person perceives a stimulus depends upon the nature of that stimulus and how the person interprets it. If the stimulus presented is relatively unstructured, vague, and equivocal, the person's interpretations of that stimulus presumably reflect aspects of his personality. That is, if the response is not determined by the stimulus itself, it presumably represents a projection on the part of the person making the response. *Example:* A series of unstructured ink blots are presented and the person is asked to describe what he sees. Suppose that, for every ink blot presented, the person "sees" a fight going on. One might infer that this reflects this person's concern with fighting or hostility.

Random Sample

A sample in which every member of a population has an equal chance of being selected for the group studied. In fact, few samples selected in research are truly random. Practicality and convenience usually enter into sampling decisions. *Example:* A researcher wishes to study high school students' perceptions of their teachers. Theoretically, the population comprises all high school students in the world, or perhaps all American high school students. Thus, assuming an American population, every high school student in the country should have an equal chance of being selected if the sample is to be truly random. In fact, the sample is more likely to depend upon where the researcher works, his contacts in the high schools, and the cooperation of school administrators, teachers, and students. Within these limits, however, the investigator could choose a random sample of 100, for example, by assigning a number to all students who might possibly participate, and then select the first 100 whose numbers occur in a table of random numbers.

Randomization

A technique for controlling intersubject or situational differences relevant to the variables studied in a research. That is, the researcher randomly assigns subjects to different groups or randomly varies certain situational variables so that there is no consistent bias introduced by intersubject or situational differences. *Example:* A researcher wishes to compare the moods of patients in two different hospitals. Patients might show consistent differences in mood as a function of the time of day; moods might tend to be more positive in the morning than they are in the afternoon. Therefore, if all the data for one hospital were collected in the morning, and all the data for the second hospital collected in the afternoon, the differences obtained might reflect the difference in time of day rather than the hospitals. One way of dealing with this problem is by randomization of the times during the day when data are collected in the two hospitals. Using a table of random numbers, the researcher would construct a schedule of data collection in the two hospitals that would not involve any consistent bias. Thus, any differences between the two hospitals could not be interpreted as a reflection of the time of day the data were collected. Another way to deal with this problem, of course, would be to counterbalance the times of the day in which data are collected in the two hospitals.

Reliability

The degree to which a measure yields consistent responses. There are three major types of reliability typically considered in psychological and educational research: (1) stability over time, usually evaluated by the correlation of scores obtained at one time with scores obtained for the same individuals a second time, after a relatively short interval; (2) interval consistency, evaluated by the correlations among items or parts of a test; and (3) observer, rater, scorer reliability, evaluated by degree of agreement among raters, judges, etc. *Example:* A researcher constructs a 20-item test designed to measure interest in education. The homogeneity of the items or internal consistency of the test might be evaluated by correlating scores obtained for the even-numbered items with scores obtained for the odd-numbered items. The temporal stability of the test might be evaluated by a test-retest procedure, correlating scores obtained one time with scores for the same individuals obtained a month later.

Replication

Repeating a study to determine whether the same results are obtained the second time. Replication of research is an important check in scientific investigation. In describing the procedures of any research, therefore, the description must be explicit enough so that another researcher can replicate the study.

Response Set

The tendency to respond in one particular way regardless of the content of the items. *Example:* A researcher develops a 30-item measure of extracurricular interests among college students. The students are required to answer *Yes* or *No* to each item. The researcher finds that some students answer *Yes* to every item; other students answer *No* to every item. This may be a function of so-called "Yea-saying" or "Nay-saying" response sets. The researcher then revises the questionnaire so that the students rate each of the 30 items on a seven-point scale, indicating their degree of interest in each activity. It is found that some students rate every item in the middle of the scale (a rating of 4). This may be a function of a response set to use the middle of any scale rather than the extremes.

Sample

Any subset or portion of a population of individuals or objects having some common characteristic. Rarely, if ever, does a study include an entire population; rather, research deals with samples, and various inferential statistics are used to aid the researcher in deciding whether results obtained for a sample can confidently be generalized to the population from which the sample comes. (See *Population*)

Sampling Distribution

The distribution of a statistic obtained for all possible samples of a given size from a particular population. The sampling distribution of a statistic (e.g., sampling distribution of the mean or of the variance) is used in inferential statistics as a basis for estimating the probability of obtaining a specific value. *Example:* Reading scores are obtained for the population of 200 students in a school. Samples of 20 students are drawn from this population, and the mean reading score of each sample is computed. The sampling distribution of means would consist of the distribution of mean scores obtained for all possible samples of 20 obtained from this population. Obviously, an enormous number of means would be involved in such a distribution; fortunately, there are mathematical ways of estimating this distribution with reasonable accuracy, without going through all the arithmetic required to compute the actual sampling distribution.

Significance Level

The probability of obtaining a given result by chance. *Example:* Using a *t*-test, a researcher compares the mean scores of two groups on a spelling test. He or she obtains a *t*-value of 3.17 and concludes that the difference is statistically significant at the .05 level. This means that there are 5 chances in 100 that the two groups don't really differ. That is, the results could occur by chance 5 times in 100. In most psychological and educational research, the investigator is willing to risk this level of chance in concluding that a difference does exist. (See *Type I error, Type II error*)

Significance Test

Various inferential statistics used to determine whether results obtained are likely to differ from chance expectations. *Examples:* *t*-test, analysis of variance, chi square, etc. (See *Inferential Statistics*)

Sociometric Techniques

A set of techniques for investigating relationships among members of a given group. *Example:* A teacher wishes to know who is friendly with whom among students. He or she might use a sociometric technique by asking each student to list the three other students in the class they would invite to a party. On the basis of these data, it would be possible to determine the rank order of frequency with which each child is chosen, who chooses whom, reciprocal and nonreciprocal choices, etc.

Spurious Relationships

A relationship obtained as a consequence of factors other than those the researcher believes are operating. *Example:* A researcher investigating the effect of introducing new and presumably better lighting in the classroom on student achievement finds that, after new lights are put in a classroom, student achievement goes up. The conclusion is that better lighting in the classroom increases student achievement. But this might be a spurious relationship. Perhaps the increased achievement was a result of the special attention paid to this particular class. (See *Hawthorne Effect*)

Standard Deviation

One of the most frequently used measures of variability. Specifically, it is the positive square root of the variance. In most studies, the mean and standard deviation are used to describe the distribution of a variable. (See *Variance*)

Standard Score

The deviation of a score from the mean of a distribution expressed in units of the standard deviation for that distribution. Translating scores in this way provides a basis for interpreting any particular score in terms of how much it differs from the mean. It allows us to compare scores from test to test. *Example:* Suppose the mean of a distribution is 80, and the standard deviation is 5. A raw score of 85 translated into a standard score ould be 1 (80—80 divided by the standard deviation of 5). Sometimes, to liminate negative values and also to standardize the standard deviation nit, a mean standard score of 50 is set with a standard deviation unit of 0. (Other values, of course, might be chosen.) For the example above, this ould entail multiplying the value obtained by 10 and adding 50, for a tandard score of 60. The general formula for a standard score with mean f 50 and standard deviation of 10 is:

$$50 + 10 \left(\frac{\text{Raw Score} - \text{Mean Score}}{\text{Standard Deviation}} \right)$$

Statistical Control

Eliminating the effects of a variable by means of statistical analysis. *Example:* A researcher compares three different ways of teaching long division in terms of the amount learned, measured by a final examination. The core on this examination is likely to be influenced by how much the students knew before the experiment started, however. Therefore, the students re given an arithmetic test before the experiment starts, and this variable s statistically controlled by an analysis of covariance.

Statistical Inference

Drawing inferences from the sample to the population. If researchers eal with the total population in which they are interested, statistical inference is obviously not required. Any difference observed *is* a difference in he population. But researchers rarely deal with the entire population. Almost always, they deal with a sample, and they need some systematic basis or deciding whether they can generalize their findings with the sample to he population they are interested in. Thus, techniques of statistical inference play an important role in the researcher's decision-making about the esults obtained. *Examples:* A *t*-test provides a basis for deciding whether he difference in means between two groups is large enough to warrant generalizing to the population sampled. A chi square provides a basis for eciding whether the observed difference in the distribution of responses iven by two or more groups is large enough to infer a real difference in he population.

Stratification

Dividing a sample into parts on the basis of some characteristic. In electing a sample to be studied, a researcher may wish to be sure that ertain characteristics of a population are represented in his sample. Therefore, he or she would first divide the population into the categories o stratifications he wanted represented, and then randomly sample subject from these subgroups. *Example:* A researcher knows that about 25 percen of a school population comes from a high socioeconomic class background 50 percent from the middle class, and 25 percent from the lower class. Th investigator wants the sample to be representative of the socioeconomi status of students in the population. Therefore, he or she first divides th student population on the basis of socioeconomic class, and then randomly selects within each class so that the proportions in the sample are the sam as those in the population. This is a stratified random sample.

t-test

A statistical inference technique used, for example, to evaluate th significance of the difference between the means of two groups. *Example* A researcher measures the height of a sample of 13-year-old boys and of sample of 13-year-old girls. He or she obtains the mean and standard devia tion for each group and then computes a t-value to determine whether th null hypothesis that there is no difference in height between 13-year-old boy and girls can be rejected. (See *Statistical Inference*)

Type I Error

Sometimes referred to as an α type error. Rejecting the null hypothesi when, in fact, it is true. The probability of a Type I error is set by the leve of significance at which the researcher decides to reject the null hypothesis *Example:* A researcher computes a chi square and obtains a value of 3.84 with one degree of freedom. This is significant at the .05 level, and the nul hypothesis is rejected. However, the investigator runs the risk of making Type I Error 5 times in 100. (See *Significance Level*)

Type II Error

Sometimes referred to as β type error. Accepting the null hypothesis when it is false and a specific alternative is true—that is, when there is real difference in the populations. For a given sample size, reducing th level of significance at which the null hypothesis will be rejected (e.g., from .05 to .01) increases the chance of a Type II Error. One way to decrease the chances of both Type I and Type II Errors is to increase the sample size. *Example:* A researcher performs a t-test comparing the means of two groups and obtains a t-value of 1.80. The conclusion is that the difference is not statistically significant, and thus the researcher does not reject the null hypothesis. If there is, in fact, a real difference between these groups in the population sampled, the researcher is making a Type II Error. (See *Type I Error*)

Validity

The degree to which a measure actually measures what it is supposed to measure. *Example:* A researcher is interested in investigating the relationship between anxiety and learning. A questionnaire measure of anxiety is developed. The validity of that questionnaire depends upon the degree to which it in fact measures anxiety. For various ways of evaluating a measure's validity, see *Concurrent validity, Construct validity, Content validity, Predictive validity.*

Variance

A measure of variability. Specifically, for a sample it is the sum of squares of the deviation of the observations from the mean, divided by one less than the total number of observations. Commonly computed to obtain the standard deviation, the positive square root of the variance, which is frequently used to describe the variability of observations in a distribution. Variance also enters into computation of various tests of statistical inference, such as the analysis of variance or covariance. (See *Standard Deviation*)

REFERENCES

American Psychological Association. *Publication manual of the American Psychological Association,* 2nd ed. Washington, D.C.: APA, 1974. *(writing research reports)*

American Psychological Association. *Standards for educational and psychological tests.* Washington, D.C.: APA, 1974. *(evaluation and measurement)*

American Psychological Association Ad Hoc Committee on Ethical Standards in Psychological Research. *Ethical principles in the conduct of research with human participants.* Washington, D.C.: APA, 1973. *(ethical considerations)*

Anastasi, A. *Psychological testing,* 4th ed. New York: Macmillan, 1976. *(evaluation and measurement)*

Anderson, S. B.; Ball, S.; & Murphy, R. T., eds. *Encyclopedia of educational evaluation.* San Francisco: Jossey-Bass, 1974. *(evaluation and measurement)*

Ary, D.; Jacobs, L. C.; & Razavich, A. *Introduction to research in education.* New York: Holt, Rinehart and Winston, 1972. *(general research methods)*

Babbie, E. R. *Survey research methods.* Belmont: Wadsworth Publishing Co., 1973. *(general research methods)*

Barzun, J.; & Graff, H. F. *The modern researcher,* 3rd ed. New York: Harcourt Brace Jovanovich, 1977. *(general research methods)*

Baumrind, D. Some thoughts on ethics of research: after reading Milgram's "Behavioral study of obedience." *American Psychologist,* 1971, *26,* 887-896. *(ethical considerations)*

Best, J. W. *Research in education,* 3rd ed. Englewood Cliffs: Prentice-Hall, 1977. *(general research methods)*

Borg, W. R.; & Gall, M. D. *Educational research: an introduction.* New York: David McKay, 1971. *(general research methods)*

Campbell, D. T.; & Stanley, J. C. *Experimental and quasi-experimental designs for research.* Chicago: Rand McNally, 1966. *(research design and planning)*

Campbell, W. G. *Form and style in thesis writing,* 3rd ed. Boston: Houghton Mifflin, 1969. *(writing research reports)*

Carlsmith, J. M.; Ellsworth, P. C.; & Aronson, E. *Methods of research in social psychology.* Reading, Mass.: Addison-Wesley, 1976. *(general research methods)*

Chase, C. J. *Measurement for educational evaluation.* Reading, Mass.: Addison-Wesley, 1974. *(evaluation and measurement)*

Cooley, W. W. Data processing and computing. In Ebel, R. J., ed., *Encyclopedia of educational research,* 4th ed. New York: Macmillan, 1969. Pp. 283-291. *(statistics and computers)*

Edwards, A. L. *Experimental design in psychological research,* 4th ed. New York: Holt, Rinehart and Winston, 1972. *(research design and planning)* uilford, J. P.; & Fruchter, B. *Experimental statistics in psychology and education*, 4th ed. New York: McGraw-Hill, 1973. (*statistics and computers*)

ollander, M.; & Wolfe, D. *Nonparametric statistical methods*. New York: John Wiley & Sons, 1975. (*statistics and computers*)

acobson, P. E., Jr. *Introduction to statistical measures for the social and behavioral sciences*. Hinsdale, Ill.: Dryden Press, 1976. (*statistics and computers*)

ohnson, M. C. *A review of research methods in education*. Chicago: Rand McNally, 1977. (*general research methods*)

elman, H. C. *A time to speak: on human values and social research*. San Francisco: Jossey-Bass, 1968. (*ethical considerations*)

eppel, G. *Design and analysis: a researcher's handbook*. Englewood Cliffs: Prentice-Hall, 1973. (*research design and planning*)

erlinger, F. N. *Foundations of behavioral research*, 2nd ed. New York: Holt, Rinehart and Winston, 1973. (*general research methods*)

ester, J. D. *Writing research papers: a complete guide*, 2nd ed. Glenview: Scott, Foresman, 1976. (*writing research reports*)

indman, H. R. *Analysis of variance in complex experimental designs*. San Francisco: W. H. Freeman, 1974. (*research design and planning*)

iller, A. G. *The social psychology of psychological research*. New York: The Free Press, 1972. (*research design and planning*)

eale, J. M.; & Liebert, R. M. *Science and behavior: an introduction to methods of research*. Englewood Cliffs: Prentice-Hall, 1973. (*general research methods*)

unnally, J. C. *Introduction to statistics for psychology and education*. New York: McGraw-Hill, 1975. (*statistics and computers*)

obin, D. *Delay of gratification in children*. Unpublished doctoral dissertation, Columbia University, 1966.

osenthal, B.; & Rosnow, R., eds. *Artifact in behavioral research*. New York: Academic Press, 1969. (*research design and planning*)

ude, P. A.; & Page, J. A. *Introduction to computers*. New York: McGraw-Hill, 1974. (*statistics and computers*)

trunk, W., Jr.; & White, E. B. *The elements of style*, 2nd ed. New York: Macmillan, 1973. (*writing research reports*)

horndike, R. L.; & Hagen, E. *Measurement and evaluation in psychology and education*, 4th ed. New York: John Wiley & Sons, 1977. (*evaluation and measurement*)

urabian, K. L. *A manual for writers of term papers, theses, and dissertations*, 4th ed. Chicago: University of Chicago Press, 1973. (*writing research reports*)

nited States Public Health Service. *Protection of the individual as a research subject*. Washington, D.C.: Government Printing Office, 1969. (*ethical considerations*)

alker, H. M.; & Lev, J. *Elementary statistical methods*, 3rd ed. New York: Holt, Rinehart and Winston, 1969. (*statistics and computers*)

iner, B. J. *Statistical principles in experimental design*, 2nd ed. New York: McGraw-Hill, 1971. (*research design and planning*)

right, R. L. D. *Understanding statistics: an informal introduction for the behavioral sciences*. New York: Harcourt Brace Jovanovich, 1976. (*statistics and computers*)

There are no rules governing the form and content of a research proposal. The material that should be covered and the most effective way of presenting relevant information always depend upon the particular research being planned. Nevertheless, there are certain conventions that might be useful to consider in preparing the outline of a research proposal.

It is usually helpful to the reader to start with a brief statement of the overall purpose of the research, in two or three lines giving the reader some idea of the general area of investigation and the particular focus of the study to be presented. This is followed by a statement of the logic of the study, which may be presented in a few paragraphs, and rarely exceeds a few pages. The emphasis in this section is on the rationale underlying the proposal, with appropriate discussion of the theoretical and empirical background out of which the research grows. The aim here is to place the proposal within the context of a line of inquiry, clarifying the reasoning or hunches that led to this specific study, and citing previous work wherever relevant. The literature is not appropriately reviewed simply by enumerating previous studies; rather, the relevant literature is used to develop the logic and background of the proposed investigation.

The logic of a proposal leads to the questions or hypotheses that are the specific focus of the study. These must be stated with great care because the rest of the proposal derives from the statement of these central questions or hypotheses.

The next major section in the proposal describes the empirical methods used to test the hypotheses or investigate the questions posed. Stating the general design of the investigation, briefly summarizing the research model to be followed, is frequently a good way to begin this section. This serves as an introduction to the more detailed description of methods and procedures that will be used.

The methods and procedures of a proposed research should be pre nted with enough concrete detail so that other trained investigators could llow the research plan. This means that a step-by-step description of the rocedures should be presented, every variable defined operationally, the bjects and the sampling techniques described carefully, and the methods r controlling relevant variables made explicit and concrete.

At the time a proposal is made, further preliminary work may need to e done to develop a specific technique or to obtain information concerning e choice of alternative techniques. The steps in this preliminary work ust be described as fully and completely as the methods and procedures f the main investigation.

The empirical methods and procedures of the research having been iscussed in detail, the next step is to state the statistical techniques to be sed, including both the descriptive and inferential statistics. Sometimes, of urse, the choice of a statistical method cannot be specified until the data re collected, because the investigator cannot predict beforehand whether ertain assumptions underlying various statistics will be met by the data. 1 any event, the range of possible choices of statistics should be indicated nd the basis for making a final decision adequately discussed.

Finally, some discussion of possible results should be presented, relat-g the proposed study to the theoretical and research background indicated t the beginning of the proposal. In particular, the meaning of null or egative results should be considered, assuring that regardless of the direc-on of results obtained the research will be of significant scientific interest.

NOTES

NOTES

NOTES